MORE
than
THE GAME

The Tennessee Football Experience

PHOTOGRAPHS
by **ROBERT HELLER**

TEXT
by **BROOKS CLARK**

Sports Publishing L.L.C.

www.sportspublishingllc.com

MORE
than
THE GAME

The Tennessee Football Experience

Layout and design: **Robert Heller and Kenneth J. O'Brien**
Cover design: **Robert Heller and Kenneth J. O'Brien**
Photos courtesy of **Robert Heller**

ISBN: 1-58261-517-9

Sports Publishing L.L.C.
www.SportsPublishingLLC.com

The first time I experienced a University of Tennessee football game, I was amazed by the visual nature of the event. As a photographer, I could not stop shooting pictures. Masses of people, blazes of color, patterns, shadows, and details were all there for my camera. I went through roll after roll of film—all before the game began. I found myself drawn to all the activity, photographing the fans, the band, the cheerleaders, the stadium, the officials, the coaches, the players, and even the photographers covering the game.

During the past 15 years, I've spent many Saturdays at Neyland Stadium and shot thousands of photographs. I leave it to others to document the action on the field. Presented here are images that portray more than the game.

—Robert Heller

TABLE OF CONTENTS

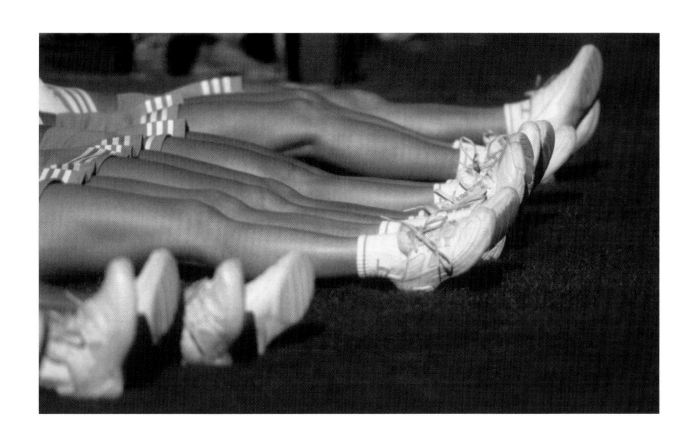

*O*ccupying just a handful of acres in Knoxville, Tennessee, becomes a city of 107,000—larger than all but four cities in the entire state.

Every spectator brings a different perspective to the games in Neyland Stadium and their surrounding pageantry, marching bands, and oceans of orange and white. Photographer Robert Heller has spent 15 years seeking the tiny moments amid the spectacle—and outside the game itself. "There's so much to be seen and learned," says Heller, "in looking with a different set of eyes at what an instant in time has to offer."

Heller's photographs range from extreme close-ups—like the silver glint of a trumpet or the back of a lineman's leg—to the study from a wide angle—the shape and order of the band, or the crowd in the stands revealed to be a unified whole, standing in identical posture, in complete concentration, of one mind.

What do Heller's photographs conjure? A revealing moment of light, when a cloud opens up and casts a sword of sunshine across a crowd. The inner feelings of one baton twirler. The awareness that college football at Tennessee exists in four dimensions. General Neyland's doctrines and legacies live and breathe in the stadium that bears his name.

THE
FANS

We always use the singular word "crowd" to describe 107,000 souls. Focused on the action on the field, this varied congregation becomes a single entity, reacting in disapproval, erupting in tumult, experiencing sentimentality, frustration, malaise—every change in emotion as palpable as a fire log in your hand.

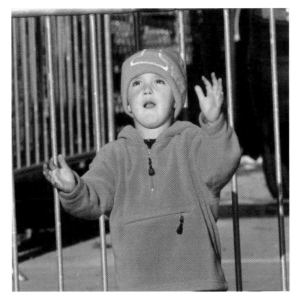

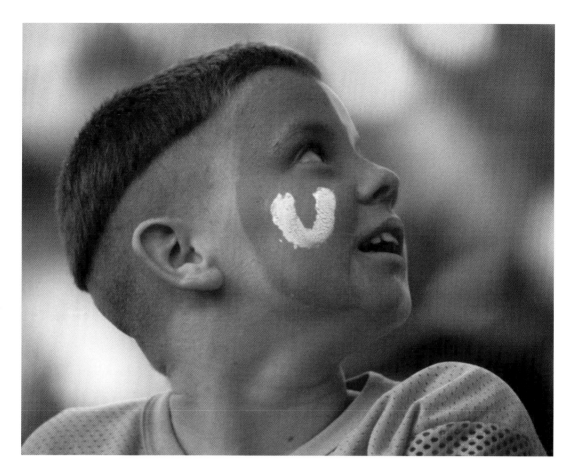

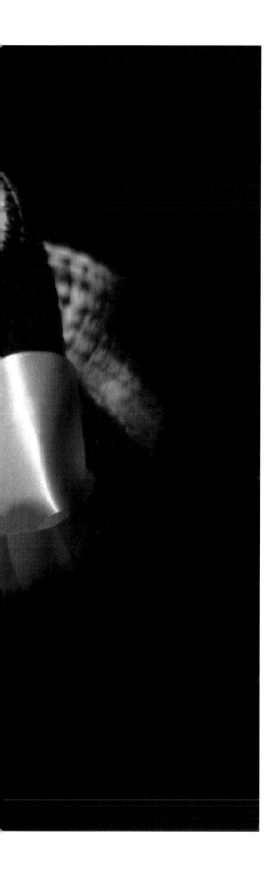

THE
BAND

Our view of the Pride of the Southland Marching Band is almost always from a distance, and we perceive mostly the large patterns of their movement. From afar we don't see the detail of the shiny black spats or

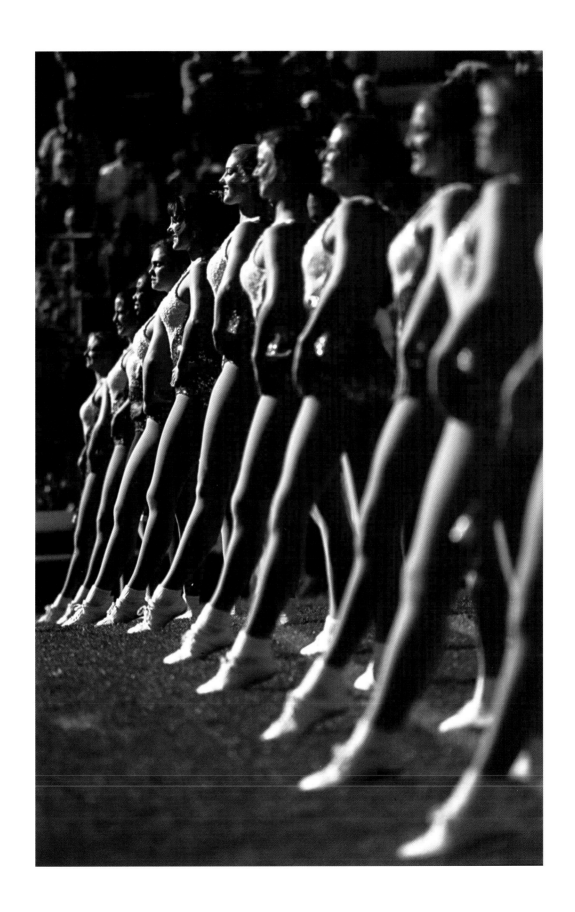

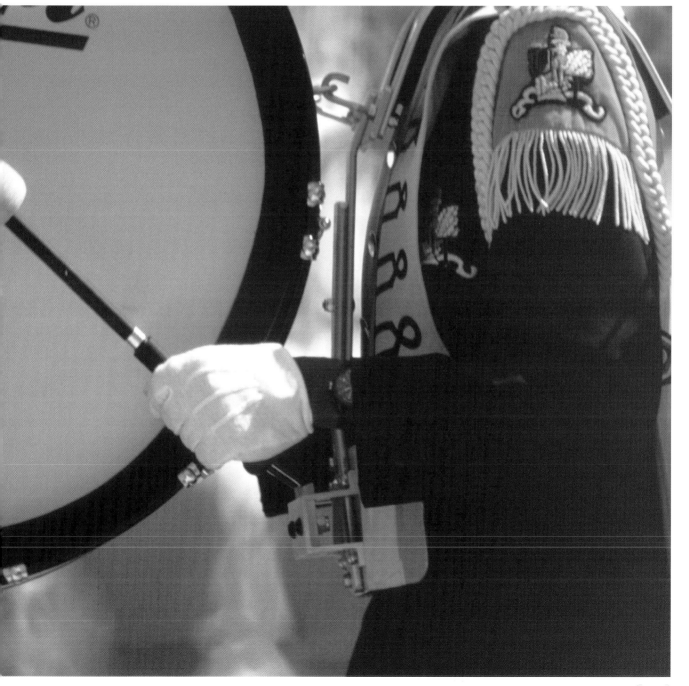

THE CHEERLEADERS

"It's like no other feeling you can talk about," says a cheerleader. "There's just nothing to compare to it."
The squads of cheerleaders are on their feet for hours, and even their moments of relaxation are orchestrated. During interludes, the boys drop to one knee and the girls perch on the outstretched thigh. Lined up in their identical poses, the pairs of cheerleaders look like porcelain figurines on a shelf.

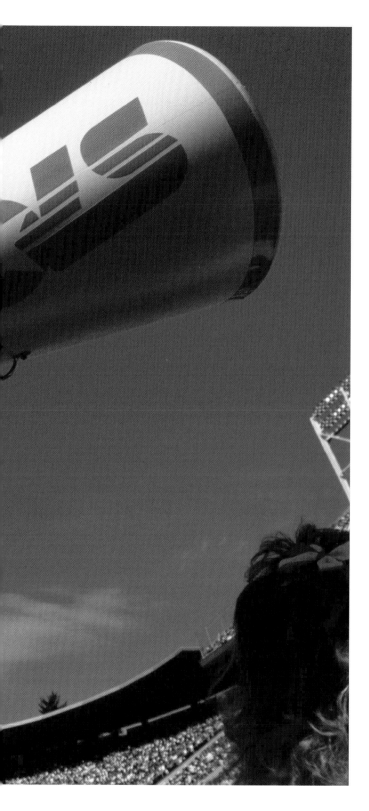

THE STADIUM

Every structure has its own character, but in our sports edifices, this flows over into something much larger. Each great stadium has a feeling, a mood, a reputation. Oh, yes—Neyland Stadium's 107,000 capacity puts it on an elite level with Michigan Stadium and the Rose Bowl, with their six-figure seating capacities. But to walk through the tunnels of Neyland—and onto the soft, manicured turf of Shields Watkins Field—is to step into timelessness. In these walls and girders and ramps and rows and sections, history blows back and forth in the present. Here's a muggy breath of air from the '92 Heath Shuler–inspired win over Florida in the deluge. And

here's a breeze from the Peyton Manning era. And now a muggy puff from Tee Martin's 1998 midnight undoing of the Gators. From the '30s, the '50s, it doesn't matter—UT football history is as alive as any re-creation on a Civil War battlefield. General Neyland (pronounced KNEE-land) made Tennessee stand for a specific brand of football—drilled in the possibilities of the kicking game, disciplined in avoiding mistakes, opportunistic and savvy. Everywhere, this stadium hints that it is a holy place for college football—from the way the sun falls on its empty stands to the shadows behind its girders.

Welcome Junior Vols

THE OFFICIALS

A referee is a study in exposed ano-
nymity. Performing in the nexus of
the action. Scrutinized, criticized,
and demonized by thousands in the
stadium and millions more on
TV. Split-second judgments sec-
ond-guessed immediately by slo-mo
replays on Jumbotrons and sets at
home. Yet we rarely know a name
or recognize a face. In real life they
are businessmen, insurance men,
sales reps. On Saturdays they are
unknown by the masses. They
are simply the "Zebras," as those
in the press box like to call
them. We see them and we
don't see them. On each play
they line up in their forma-
tion, just as the teams do, but
we are unaware of them un-
til we see a flash of yellow.

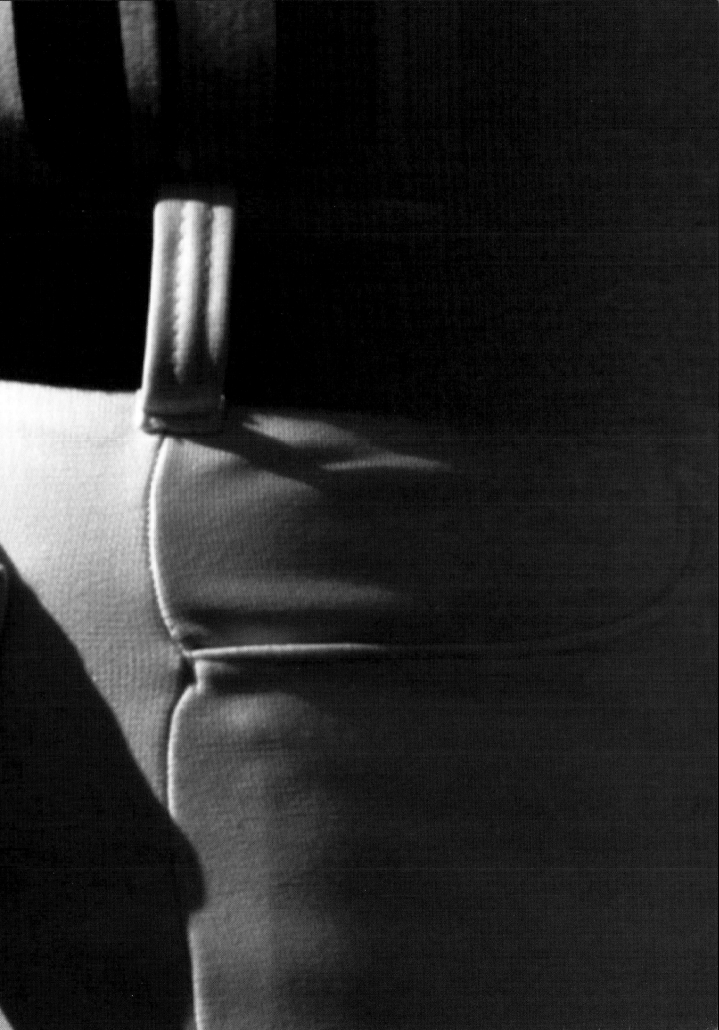

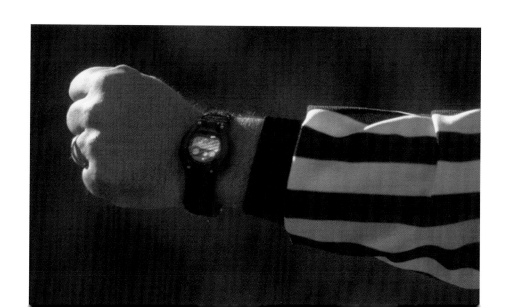

THE
PLAYERS

From afar, players look identical, like soldiers in a toy army. Up close, their uniforms reveal personal choices, individuality, and the realities of the contest. The offensive linemen squeezed into too-tight jerseys so defenders will have no fabric to grab onto. Defensive linemen's assortment of grass-stained wrist and forearm pads. The quarterback drying his fingers on his rolled-up waist towel. Mouth guards, orange plastic hot-molded to the teeth, wedged in cracks between bars of the face mask and the helmet. A day's growth or more on the faces. When a foot or ankle is injured and the socks and cleats come off on the bench, layers of tape encase the ankle in flexible armor.

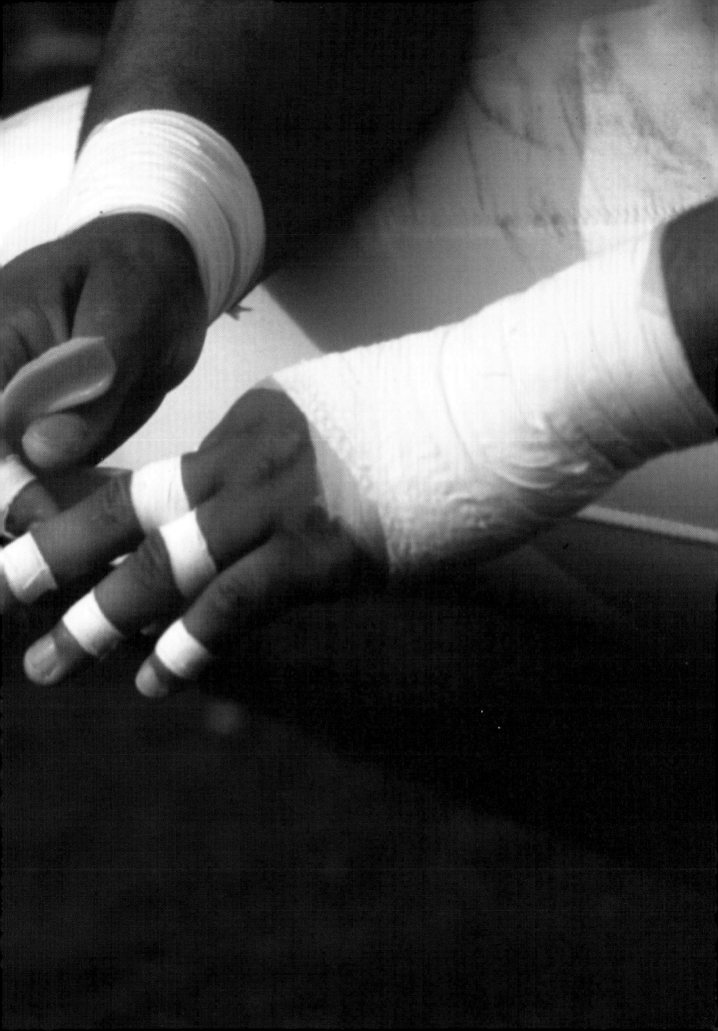

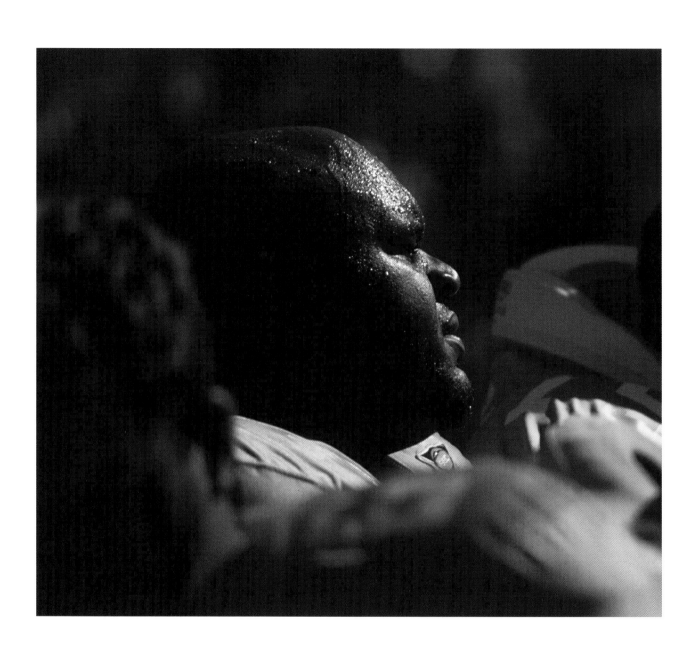

THE COACHES

Up in the press box, three coaches describe what they are seeing to their colleagues on the sideline. On the bench, five linemen watch a coach draw blocking assignments on a dry-erase board. "This defensive lineman is crashing here while another fills in over here. You" —pointing the marker— "pick him up. You" — pointing the marker again— "pick him up." Such is the intricate science, mystery to the masses, kept from all but the initiated. There's also the man on the sideline, wires coming from his headphones, conducting the symphony of action—or watching with amusement as the cacophony unfolds.

THE MEDIA

Do we ever notice the picture-takers on the field? Mostly when a player hurtles off the field and clobbers one like a bowling ball decking a tenpin. We might see the rolling TV camera if we're in lower seats. We might make passing note of a sideline sage or two talking to a shoulder-held camera. But more often than not, the media go undetected in our colosseum of action and conflict.

Photographers are capturers of isolated deeds and nanoseconds of action. For the one or two pictures used in a newspaper or a magazine, it might take dozens of rolls of film and a full day of effort—and a full understanding of what is about to happen.

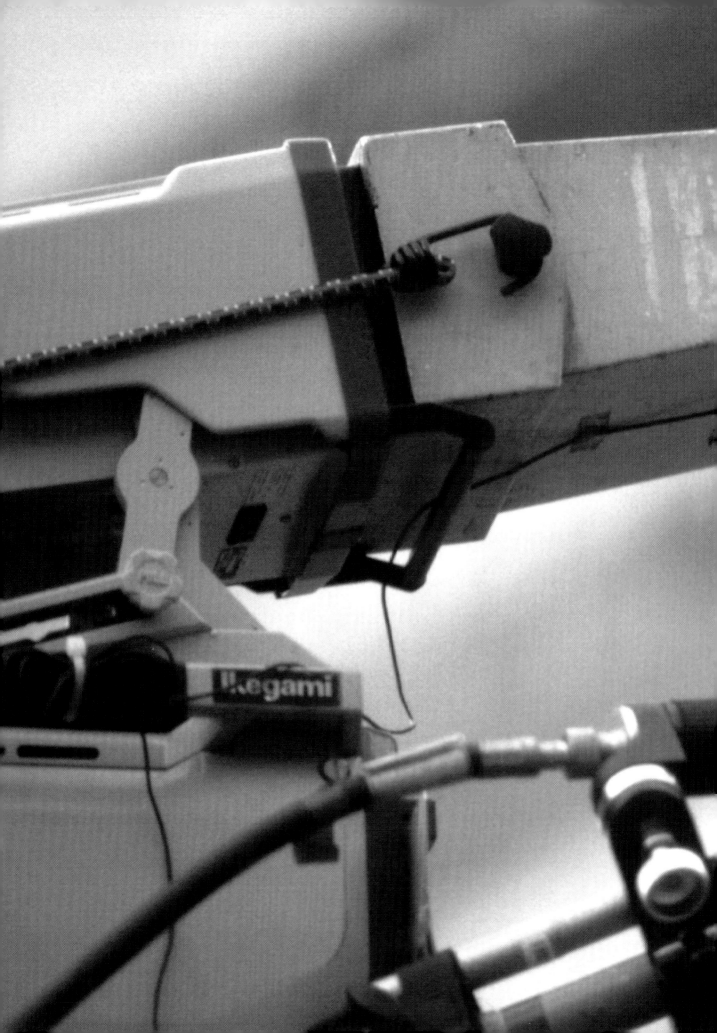

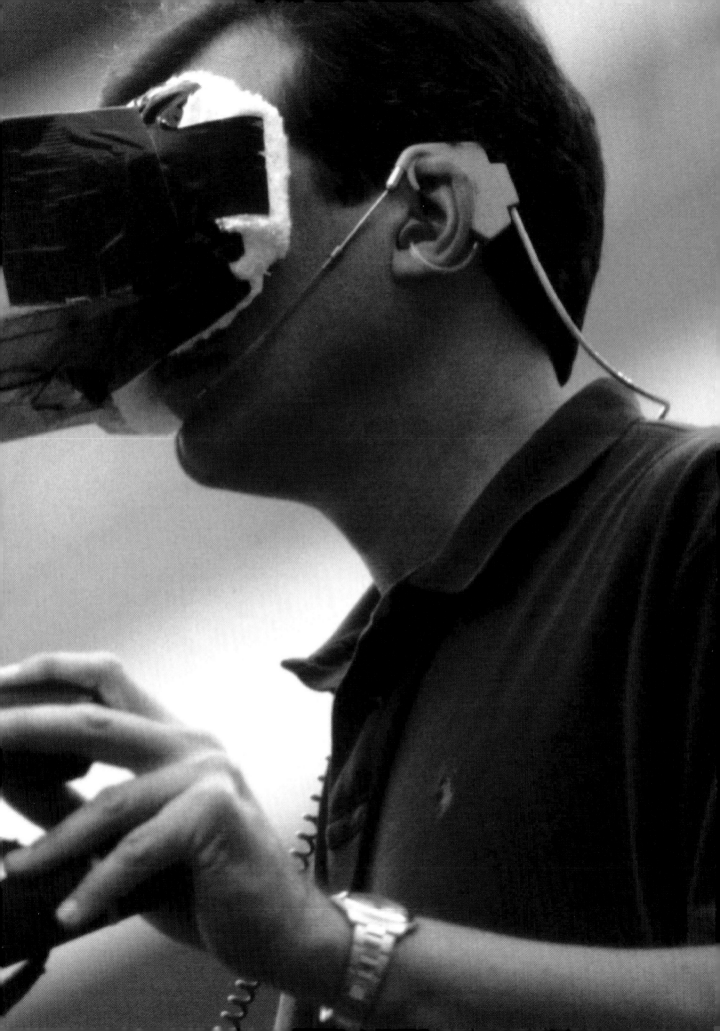

ACKNOWLEDGMENTS

Thanks to the University of Tennessee Men's Athletics Department for its courtesy in providing me with credentials to photograph at football games. Brooks Clark is a talented writer who has contributed his poetic words and ideas to this project. Director of the School of Journalism James Crook and Dean of the College of Communications Dwight Teeter have been extremely supportive of my creative work. Over the course of more than 20 years of teaching, my students have helped me keep my passion for photography alive. My parents, Milton and Dorothee Heller, have given me the right combination of genes to be successful in my career as a photographer, graphic designer and teacher. Most of all, thanks to my sons, Joel and Benjamin, for their love and support, and to my wife, Beth, who has been my inspiration in all the work that I do.